Ella and Noa Celebrate Passover

Sticker Activity Book

Use the stickers at the back of the book to bring the fun Passover scenes to life.

Illustrated by Brenda Moreno Gracia and Idit Fridman
Designed by Michal Gil

Spring

Passover happens every year at the beginning of spring.
That's why Passover is sometimes called the spring festival.
Add friends, animals and more to this beautiful spring day.

Passover Cleaning

During Passover it is forbidden to eat or own chametz.
Help Ella and Noah clean their house for Passover and find all the leftover chametz.

5

In Egypt

For hundreds of years the Israelites were forced to work very hard and build cities for Pharaoh.

Place the Israelites and Egyptians in this desert scene.

7

Saving Baby Moses

Moses's mother put him in a basket and placed him on the Nile river.
Pharaoh's daughter found him and adopted him.
Cover the river with animals and plants, and carefully place the baby
basket on the water.

The Plagues of Egypt

When Pharaoh refused to free the Israelites God sent ten plagues upon Egypt.

Blood

Wild animals

Frogs

Lice

Diseased livestock

Boils

Hail

Locusts

Darkness

Death of the first-born

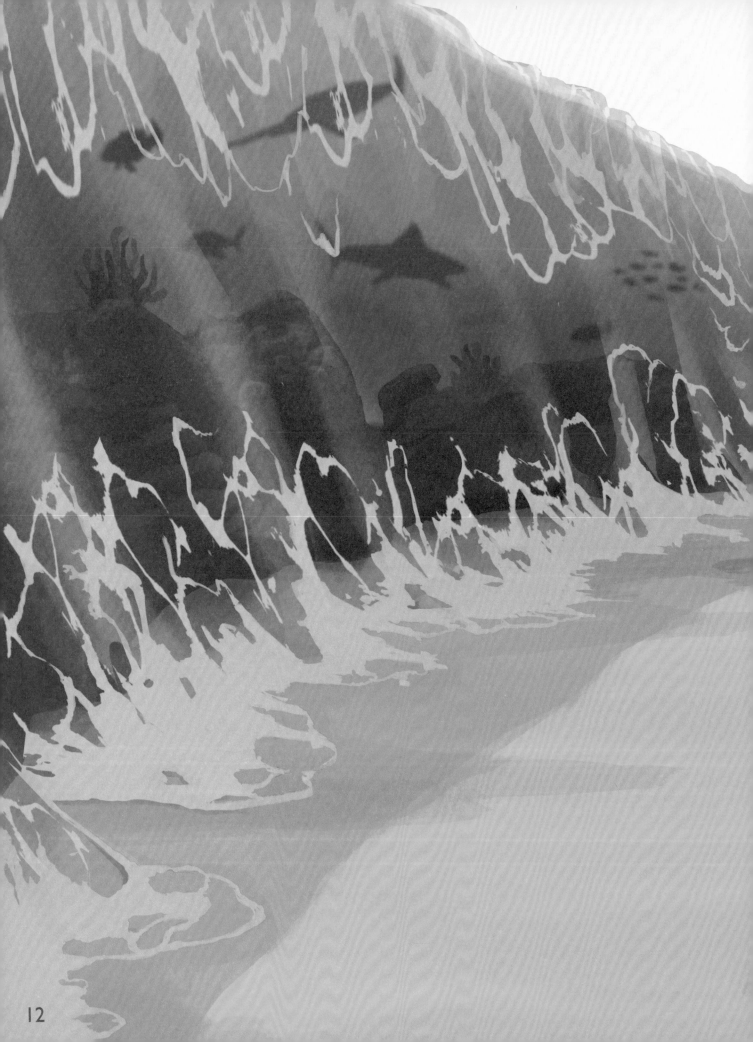

Exodus

Moses led the Israelites out of Egypt. Pharaoh's army chased after them.
Moses split the Red Sea so that the Israelites could cross safely.
Help the Israelites cross the Red Sea and flee from Pharaoh's army.

Passover Seder

We read the Haggadah around the Passover Seder table and retell the story of the Israelites' journey to freedom.
Help Ella and Noah set the Seder table with wine, flowers, plates, silverware and more. Don't forget the special Seder plate too.

Finding the Afikoman

The afikoman is the very last piece of matzah we eat at the
Passover seder. Hide it away somewhere so that Ella, Noah
and their friends can look for the afikoman!

Ten Plagues

Color the plagues so that there are two of each kind.

Blood

Wild animals

Diseased livestock

Locusts

Hail

18

Frogs

Lice

Boils

Death of the first-born

Darkness

Preparing the Passover Seder

Color in only the items you would find at the Passover Seder.

Journey to the Promised Land

Help the Israelites reach the promised land.

Spring Birds

Color in the birds so that there are two of each kind.

The Prophet Elijah

Help the prophet Elijah find the way to his cup.

In Egypt (pages 6-7)

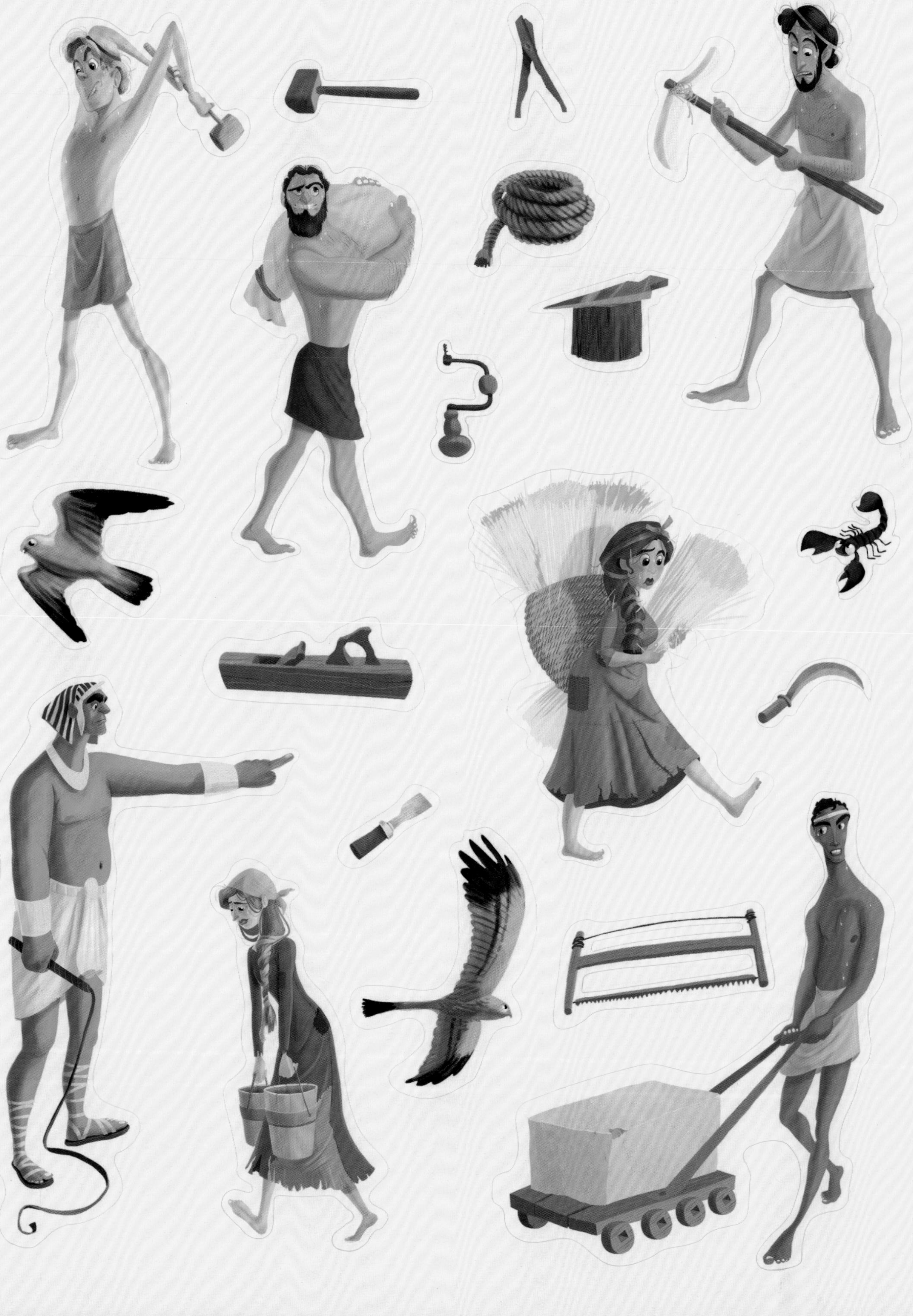

The Plagues of Egypt (pages 10-11)

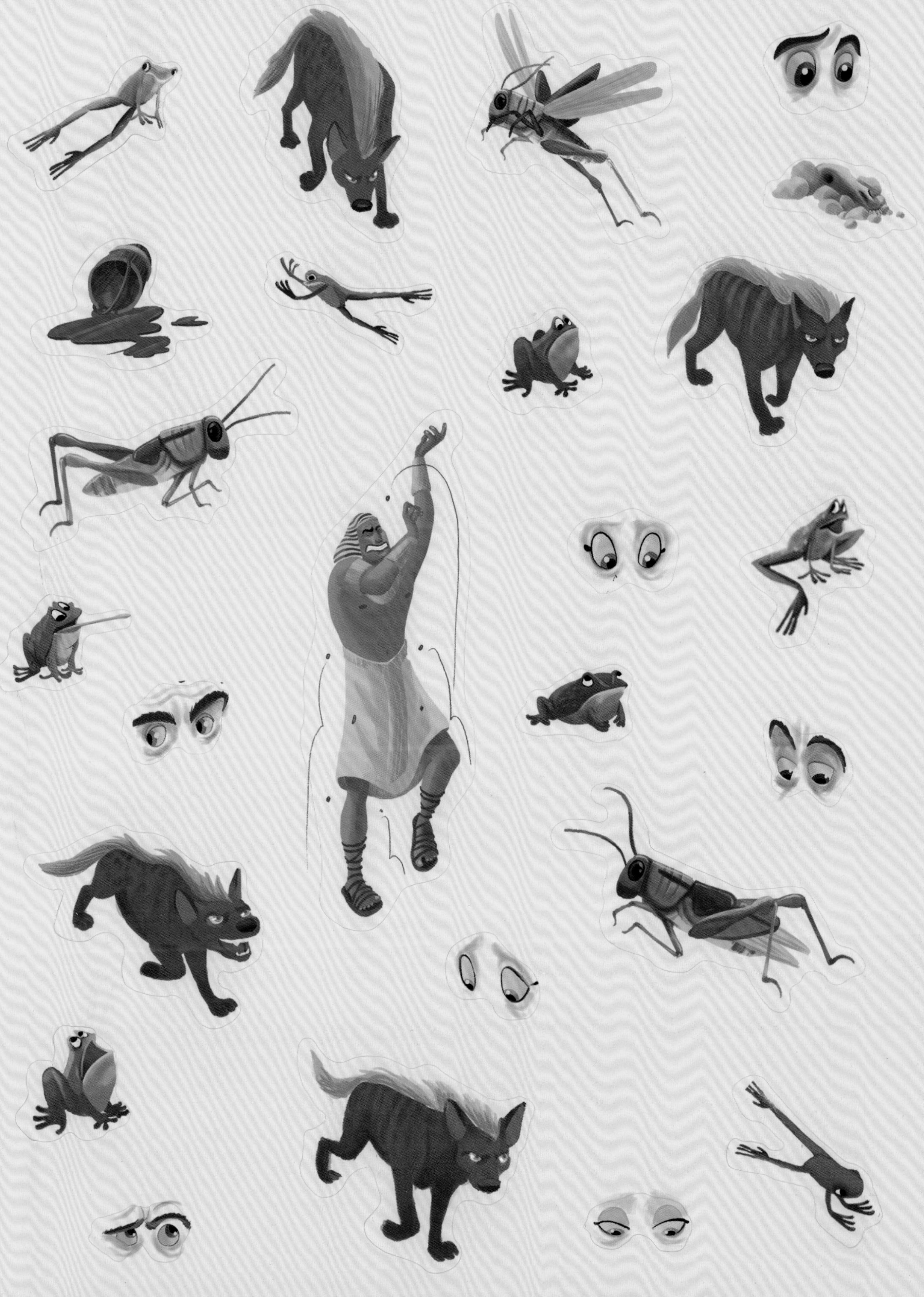